ISLAM

BULLET GUIDE

Hodder Education, 338 Euston Road, London NW1 3BH

Hodder Education is an Hachette UK company

First published in UK 2011 by Hodder Education

This edition published 2011

Copyright © 2011 Victor W. Watton

The moral rights of the author have been asserted.

Database right Hodder Education (makers)

Artworks (internal and cover): Peter Lubach
Cover concept design: Two Associates

British Library Cataloguing in Publication Data: a catalogue record for this title is available from the British Library.

10 9 8 7 6 5 4 3 2 1

The publisher has used its best endeavours to ensure that any website addresses referred to in this book are correct and active at the time of going to press. However, the publisher and the author have no responsibility for the websites and can make no guarantee that a site will remain live or that the content will remain relevant, decent or appropriate.

The publisher has made every effort to mark as such all words which it believes to be trademarks. The publisher should also like to make it clear that the presence of a word in the book, whether marked or unmarked, in no way affects its legal status as a trademark.

Every reasonable effort has been made by the publisher to trace the copyright holders of material in this book. Any errors or omissions should be notified in writing to the publisher, who will endeavour to rectify the situation for any reprints and future editions.

Hachette UK's policy is to use papers that are natural, renewable and recyclable products and made from wood grown in sustainable forests. The logging and manufacturing processes are expected to conform to the environmental regulations of the country of origin.

www.hoddereducation.co.uk

Typeset by Stephen Rowling/Springworks

Printed in Spain

ISLAM

BULLET GUIDE

Victor W. Watton

Acknowledgements

The quotations from the Qur'an are taken from – The Holy Qur'an, translation and commentary by Yusuf Ali, with permission from the publisher, Islamic Propagation Centre International, 124 Queen Street, Durban 4001, South Africa.

About the author

Victor Watton is the author of many bestselling books on religion. His particular areas of expertise are Christianity and Islam, in which his studies and research have been augmented by friendships and involvement in those communities. As well as writing, Victor spent many years as a teacher of religion in schools and colleges, and, more recently, set up (and was Chief Examiner for) some extremely popular GCSE courses: Christianity, Roman Catholic Christianity, Islam, Judaism, Hinduism, Buddhism, Sikhism, the relationship of religion to life and the impact of religion on society. Victor has been very involved in developing community cohesion in the UK since the 1970s and hopes that his writing contributes to a greater understanding between religious groups, leading to a more harmonious and peaceful multifaith community.

Contents

1 The main beliefs of Islam 1
2 Authority and guidance in Islam 13
3 Different groups in Islam 25
4 Worship and festivals 37
5 Rites of passage 49
6 Issues of life and death 61
7 Equality and rights 73
8 Creation and the environment 85
9 Practising Islam in a non-Muslim society 97
10 War, punishment and living in a multifaith society 109

Introduction

Islam is the second most popular religion in the world, with more than 1.5 billion adherents. In most Western countries Islam is the religion second to Christianity, albeit with much lower numbers than Christianity and those with no religious affiliation. In the Middle East, Central Asia and North Africa, Islam is the predominant religion.

The importance of Muslim countries for world oil supplies, and the impact of Muslim groups such as al-Qaeda and the Taleban, have made Islam a focus of interest and concern for many in the West.

Islam is one of the more recent world religions, developing in Arabia in the seventh century with the Prophet Muhammad, whose successors established a Muslim empire stretching from Spain to China within 200 years of his death. Muslim scholars would, however, claim that Islam is the oldest, indeed the original, religion, beginning with the first man, Adam, who is claimed to be the first prophet of Islam.

Islam accepts all the prophets of Judaism and Christianity as prophets of Islam whose messages were distorted by Jews and Christians so that God had to send his final prophet, Muhammad, to deliver God's true message in a way that could never be distorted.

This book gives readers an introduction to the Islamic religion to help in understanding its main beliefs and practices, the different groups within Islam and Muslim attitudes to the major issues of the modern world.

Throughout the book, Allah is used to describe God, as is preferred by Muslims. Allah is the Arabic word for the one God of Judaism and Christianity.

Common Era dates are used. Islam dates from the emigration of Muhammad from Makkah to Madinah in 622 CE, but uses a lunar calendar so that dates cannot be calculated simply by subtracting 622: for example, 2011 CE is 1432 AH (in the year of the Hijrah), not 1389 AH.

1 The main beliefs of Islam

The Six Beliefs

Muslims believe that Muhammad decreed that they must have faith in:

1 Allah
2 His angels
3 His holy books
4 His messengers
5 the Last Day
6 life after death.

These six are not the only beliefs:

* Islam means submission.
* Muslim means one who has submitted.

This means that Muslims must also follow the **Five Pillars** and the **Shari'ah**.

To be a Muslim one must accept the Six Beliefs

The Six Beliefs of Islam are usually summarized by Muslims under the following three concepts:

1 **Tawhid** (the unity of Allah) – belief in Allah.
2 **Risalah** (the messengers of Allah) – belief in angels, holy books and messengers.
3 **Akirah** (the last things) – belief in the Last Day and life after death.

We will explore these concepts in the rest of this chapter.

Some Muslims think that belief in Allah's control of everything (**Al'Qad'r**) is a seventh belief.

Allah is Arabic for 'the one God'. Muslims use it because they believe that Arabic is the language of heaven.

Tawhid

Tawhid is belief in Allah's **unity**. The word Allah has no plural form, showing that there is only one Allah.

The first part of the Muslim creed states:

I BEAR WITNESS THAT THERE IS NO GOD BUT ALLAH

4

Allah's unity means that he has no partners, no helpers and, especially, no equals. Muslims feel that the Christian belief in Trinity is an insult to Allah's unity.

Tawhid is important for Muslims because, if there is only one Allah:

* Allah must be the creator of everything.
* Allah must be all powerful and in control of everything.
* Allah must be present in the universe he has created.

The consequences of Tawhid are:

* Muslims must try to preserve the oneness of nature.
* The Muslim community must be a unity (this is called the **ummah**).
* There can be only one law, Allah's law, the Shari'ah.
* Only one Allah can be worshipped and the worst sin (**shirk**) is to associate others with Allah.
* There can be no images or statues in the mosque.

Risalah

Muslims believe that the **unity and greatness** of Allah mean that he cannot communicate directly with humans.

Allah created the **angels** as immortal beings with no free will so that they would be sinless and do Allah's will. As they are **sinless**, angels can have direct contact with Allah and pass his messages to humans.

Muslims believe that **Satan** was an angel who refused to acknowledge Adam's superiority and so was cast out of heaven.

It is angels who record the good and bad deeds of humans and present them to Allah on the **Last Day.** The chief angel is **Jibril** (Gabriel), who gives Allah's message to the prophets.

Why do we need prophets?

Muslims believe that Allah created humans to look after the earth for him (Allah's **khalifahs** or vicegerents) and we need prophets to know how to do this.

Did Islam begin with Muhammad?

Muslims believe that Islam began with the creation of humans, and so it is the original religion begun by Allah and his first prophet, Adam.

Are prophets angels?

Islam teaches that the prophets were all ordinary human beings – what made them different was that they were chosen to receive Allah's messages.

Most Muslims believe that it is wrong to treat prophets in the same way that Christians treat Jesus.

Muslims believe that Islam is the first religion

The prophets

The main prophets are:

Adam	The first man and the first prophet after he confessed his sins. He built the first **Ka'aba** in Makkah (a cube-shaped building in the centre of the Great Mosque)
Ibrahim (Abraham)	Rejected polytheism and became a Muslim. He was given the holy book The Scrolls of Ibrahim
Musa (Moses)	Took the Jews from Egypt to the Promised Land and was given the holy book Tawrat (Torah)
Dawud (David)	The great King of Israel. He was given the holy book Zabur (Psalms)
Isa (Jesus)	Had a virgin birth and performed miracles. He was given the holy book Injil (Gospel). He did not die, but was taken to heaven from the cross
Muhammad	The final prophet (570–632 CE), who established Islam in Arabia

Why is Muhammad so important?

The message of the prophets was distorted or forgotten, so Allah sent Muhammad with:

* a message that could not be distorted
* a holy book (the Qur'an), which could never be distorted.

So, Muhammad is:

* the final prophet – there will never be another
* the seal of the prophets – he sums up Allah's messages
* the final example of how humans should live.

Why is the Qur'an so important?

Muslims believe that the Qur'an:

* is the final word of Allah given to Muhammad
* is an earthly copy of a heavenly original
* tells humans what to believe and how to behave.

Akirah

The Last Day

Muslims believe that this world will be brought to an end by Allah on a day of his choosing:

* Isa (Jesus) will return.
* The angel Israfil will sound the trumpet.
* The world will disappear.
* The dead will be raised.
* Everyone will stand before Allah on the plain of Arafat (near Makkah).
* Everyone will be judged by Allah.
* Good Muslims will go to heaven.
* Bad Muslims and non-Muslims will go to hell.

Heaven and hell

Heaven is believed to be a garden of delight. Hell is believed to be a place of fire and horrors. The beliefs about the Last Day and the afterlife mean that Muslims try to live good Muslim lives to avoid hell:

* They observe the Five Pillars of Islam.
* They eat halal food and observe Muslim dress laws.
* They do not drink alcohol, gamble or lend or borrow money at interest.

Nothing should be removed from the body after death, as the body needs to be raised, so they try to avoid postmortems and many have concerns about transplant surgery.

2 Authority and guidance in Islam

Authority and the Qur'an

Muslims believe that the Qur'an:

* is the direct revelation of Allah
* is a part of Allah in the world.

Consequently, it is the basis of all authority. A secondary source is the things Muhammad said (**hadith**).

Guidance for Muslims comes from the **Shari'ah**, a set of laws for living a good life based on the Qur'an and hadith.

The Qur'an is the basis of all authority for Muslims

This chapter looks at the sources of authority and guidance for Muslims.

This is the Book, in it is guidance sure without doubt to those who fear Allah.

Sura 2:2

Muslims believe in the authority of the Qur'an because they believe that:

* It is Allah's actual, final words.
* It was revealed to Muhammad in such a way that it cannot be distorted.
* It tells humans all they need to know.

They believe in the truth of the Qur'an because:

* There is only one version – every copy is the same.
* It was revealed over a short period of time.
* Muhammad could not have made it up as he was illiterate.

The Qur'an and the hadith

How do Muslims treat the Qur'an?

Muslims believe that the Arabic Qur'an is Allah's words, and therefore the holiest thing they can possess. So:

* They keep it wrapped up.
* They never touch it without first washing their hands.
* They never eat, drink or chat while holding it.
* They read it on special stands.

All Muslims must learn to read the Qur'an in Arabic.

Some Muslims learn the Qur'an off by heart and are called **hafiz**.

Muslims in non-Arabic countries can read the words but often do not understand them.

What are hadith and why are they important?

Hadith are things that Muhammad is recorded as having said.

There are several collections of hadith, but the two that most Muslims accept as genuine are:

1 Hadith of Bukhari
2 Hadith of Sahih Muslim.

These are regarded as genuine because they have a line of guarantors going back to a companion of the prophet who heard Muhammad say them.

Hadith are second in importance to the Qur'an because Muslims believe that:

✳ Muhammad was the final prophet so his words must be important.
✳ The best person to interpret the Qur'an must be Muhammad.
✳ If the Qur'an is not clear, one must follow hadith.
✳ Hadith are one of the bases of the Shari'ah.

For Muslims, Allah's law should be the only law

The Shari'ah

Muhammad established Islam as a religious community in Medina; consequently, Muhammad's laws were both the law of the state and the religious law. So the Shari'ah:

* should be the only law for Muslims
* is Allah's law
* is the way all Muslims should live.

The Shari'ah is based on:

1 the Qur'an and the example and sayings of Muhammad (**sunna** and **hadith**)
2 secondary sources such as **consensus, custom** and **analogy**.

Some Muslim countries use the Shari'ah as state law – for example Saudi Arabia and Iran.

Some Muslim countries use the Shari'ah only for family law – for example Morocco.

Some Muslim countries have given up the Shari'ah – for example Turkey.

Why are there different law schools?

During debate throughout the first four centuries of Islam, four **Sunni** law schools emerged:

1 **Hanifite School** (Turkey, Central Asia, India, Pakistan) uses analogy (finding a similar situation in the Qur'an or hadith) and opinion (decision of a Muslim lawyer).
2 **Malikite School** (North and West Africa) uses custom (what happened in **Madinah**, city of the Prophet) and consensus (agreement of Muslim lawyers and leaders).
3 **Shafi'ite School** (Middle East, Indonesia, Malaysia, East Africa) uses consensus and analogy.
4 **Hanbalite School** (Arabia) does not use secondary sources.

Shi'a Muslims have their own **Shi'a School** (Iran, Iraq), which uses hadith of **Ali** (Muhammad's son-in-law) and the opinions of **ayatollahs** (religious leaders).

Religious laws

As Islam is a religion with a holy law, there are actions that are lawful (**halal**) and those that are banned (**haram**). There are also actions that are disapproved of but not banned (**makruh**).

This can be seen in attitudes to food and drink.

Halal	Haram	Makruh
The meat of herbivores that has been slaughtered by slitting the throat, draining the blood and praying (halal butchery)	Meat that has not been slaughtered in the halal way	Tobacco
Fish and vegetables	Alcohol and drugs	
	Pork, carrion, the meat of carnivores	

There are many other things that are haram for Muslims, including gambling (including lotteries and raffles) and lending or borrowing money at interest.

What are ulamas and fatwas?

Ulama is the word used to describe a group of Muslim religious lawyers, who have the authority to:

* decide which law school a country should follow
* decide what is lawful and prohibited in new areas, e.g. computing.

Often the ulama will have a leader, who may be called a **mufti** or a **qadi**. When they make a decision, it is termed a **fatwa** to show that:

* This is a religious decision.
* This is a decision that Muslims should follow.

Attitudes to imams and authority

Most **imams** in the UK are:

* prayer leaders
* preachers of the Friday sermon
* teachers in the **madrassah** (children's mosque school)
* trained in traditional Arabic, Shari'ah and Qur'anic studies.

Imams are not the same as Christian priests and ministers. They are not ordained but employed by the committee that runs the mosque.

In non-Muslim countries, imams often take over the role of the ulama, giving them responsibility for:

* interpreting the Shari'ah for the country in which they live
* giving advice on how to live a good Muslim life in that country
* helping young Muslims to understand and keep their faith.

The Imam in Shi'ah Islam is a totally different, semi-divine figure (see Chapter 3).

22

Do all Muslims agree about authority and guidance?

Not really!

The views described in this chapter are those of traditional Muslims. However, there are two other sets of beliefs in Islam:

1 **Modernizers**, the smallest group who believe:

* Traditional Islam needs reforming to reflect the true religion.
* Hadith and the law schools cannot be trusted.
* Islam should be based only on the Qur'an.
* Women should have equal rights.
* Islam should be more related to the modern world.

2 **Fundamentalists**, the fastest growing group who believe:

* Islam should be based on the Qur'an and hadith alone.
* Men and women were created for different roles.
* The problems of the West are due to the rise of feminism.
* Women have true freedom in their Muslim role.

3 Different groups in Islam

Sunni and Shi'a

Islam should be one religion, but, within 30 years of Muhammad's death, it split into two:

* **Sunnis** – follow only the example of Muhammad.
* **Shi'a** – follow the example of Muhammad's son-in-law, Ali, as well as that of Muhammad.

Since then, different groups have formed within the Sunnis (e.g. the Taleban) and within the Shi'as (e.g. the Druze), and across Sunni and Shi'a (e.g. Sufis).

The two major groups in Islam are Sunnis and Shi'as

Why did Islam split?

When Muhammad died, many Muslims believed that Ali should be leader, as he was Muhammad's first convert and father of his grandchildren. Ali was eventually elected, but his death caused more conflict, as some Muslims wanted Ali's son to be **caliph**, but he and his followers were massacred.

Ali's followers became Shi'as, and the followers of the **Umayyad** caliphs became Sunnis.

In this chapter we will look at the divisions in Islam arising from the first split.

Exploring the differences

What are the main differences between Sunni and Shi'a?

Sunni	Shi'a
Muhammad is the final prophet with the final message. Imams are just prayer leaders	The Imam (who must be a descendant of Muhammad) receives messages from Allah
The first four caliphs were rightly guided	The first three caliphs betrayed Islam
The Qur'an is eternal and speaks directly	Allah created the Qur'an and it needs interpreting
The Twelfth Imam died	The Twelfth Imam went into hiding and will return to bring in the end of the world
	Some believe that specially able religious leaders (**ayatollahs**) are in contact with the **Hidden Imam**

28

Are there any different groups in the Shi'as?

Yes! Here are some:

1 **Twelvers** – most Shi'as believe in Twelve Imams and the Hidden Imam.

2 **Ismailis** – believe that the Seventh Imam should have been Ismail and his descendants are Imams.

3 **Nizari Khojas** – an Ismailite sect whose leader, the Aga Khan, is regarded as the Imam of the age.

4 **Druze** – believe in reincarnation, often have Christian names and do not need to follow the Five Pillars.

Many scholars believe that the Baha'i religion came from the Shi'as.

Iran is a Twelver Shi'a country, and 60% of Iraqis are Twelvers. There are substantial numbers of Shi'a in Pakistan and Yemen.

Sufism

Sufism is Islamic mysticism that:

* seeks the heart of religion
* tries to unite individuals with Allah (**fana**).

To become a Sufi a Muslim:

* joins a Sufi leader (a **shaykh** or **pir**)
* gives up possessions
* follows the leader's teachings and practices.

Rumi, a medieval Sufi, described fana thus:

'Allah makes them absent from the world when they are in union with him.'

How do Sufis relate to the rest of Islam?

Some Muslims regard the Sufis as very important because:

* They encourage Muslims to look at their relationship with Allah.
* They emphasize the value of religious experience over simply following rules.
* They give ordinary people the chance to find Allah.

Some Muslims regard Sufis as dangerous, and even non-Muslim, because:

* They think finding Allah is more important than following the Shari'ah.
* The teachings of a **shaykh** can become more important than those of the Qur'an.
* Some Sufis allow followers to ignore the Five Pillars.

Sufism is very popular in the poorest parts of the Muslim world, where it offers hope and equality. It is also popular in Western universities.

The most famous Sufis are the whirling dervishes

The Wahhabis

Who are the Wahhabis?

In the eighteenth century, Muhammad ibn Abdul Wahhab felt that Islam had become impure. He led a mission to Arabia and converted the Saud family, who established Saudi Arabia in the early twentieth century.

Wahhabi Islam is the religion of Saudi Arabia. Wahhabis believe that:

* Islam should be based solely on the Qur'an and hadith.
* Muhammad was only a man and should not be worshipped.
* Festivals connected with Muhammad should not be celebrated.
* Muslims should not celebrate birthdays, listen to music, dance, etc.
* Muslims should not worship the graves of saints or follow holy men.
* Muslims should use the **hadd** punishments (amputations, etc.).
* Photographs should not be taken or displayed.

32

What groups have come from the Wahhabis?

The **Taleban** in Afghanistan are greatly influenced by Wahhabism. They ban television, music and cinema, and girls' schools, and use the hadd punishments.

Al-Qaeda, founded by Osama bin Laden, has similar views to the Taleban, but they also want to establish an Islamic world state.

The **Deobandis** are a Pakistani group with Wahhabi beliefs but much less political, emphasizing Islam as a personal religion.

The **Tablighi Jamaat** is a more political Deobandi group, recognizable by their caps, beards and trousers shortened to above the ankles.

Explaining more differences

Are there other groups in the Sunnis?

Yes, there are!

1   The Barelvis
The main group among British Muslims, it originated in Northern India as a reaction against Wahhabism. They revere Muhammad, celebrate his birthday and have close connections with Sufism.

2   The Jamaat-I-Islami
Began as a Pakistani political party and tries to relate acceptance of the Shari'ah with a modern democratic state.

3   Modernizer groups
Try to relate Islam to Western knowledge. Examples are Ahl-e-Hadith, the Pervaizi, and the Islamic Party of Britain.

4   The Ahmadiyya
Regarded by many Muslims as non-Muslim. They believe in the equality of women and the need for Muslims to have Western education. They have their own mosques.

Are there cultural differences among Muslims?

Pakistani, Indian and Bangladeshi Muslims often observe **Biraderi.** This is similar to the Hindu concept of caste, and is quite against the Muslim teaching of the brotherhood and community of Islam.

Attitudes to dress vary from culture to culture, not only in such things as **shalwar kameez** or **burnous** but also in terms of coverage: women in Africa, India and the Far East do not cover their faces.

There are many differences in marriage customs. Pakistani and Bangladeshi weddings resemble Hindu weddings, whereas Egyptian weddings are similar to British weddings.

There are also language differences, and most mosques are organized by nationality, i.e. a Pakistani mosque, a Somali mosque, etc.

4 Worship and festivals

The Five Pillars

In this chapter we shall be looking at the Five Pillars.

Muslims believe that Islam is like a house: the foundation is the Qur'an; the Five Pillars support the roof; the roof is the Shari'ah.

The Five Pillars are:

1 **Shahadah** – declaration of faith.
2 **Salah** – ritual prayer.
3 **Zakah** – compulsory giving to the poor.
4 **Sawm** – fasting during Ramadan.
5 **Hajj** – pilgrimage to Makkah.

The Five Pillars are the basis of worship for Muslims

What is the shahadah?

This is the Muslim creed that sums up Islam.

There is no god but Allah. Muhammad is the Prophet of Allah.

What is salah?

* **Salah** is ritual prayer that must be performed five times a day.
* The time for prayer is announced by the call of the **muezzin**.
* Muslims must prepare for salah by washing and finding a clean place.
* They must then face the direction of Makkah (**qibla**).
* They must then carry out a set prayer ritual (**raka**).
* Each prayer time has a set number of rakat.
* Salah must be said in Arabic, doing the same actions and facing the same direction.

Muslims can make personal prayers (**du'a**) at any time using their own language.

Ramadan

Sawm is the Fourth Pillar and means fasting during the hours of daylight in the month of Ramadan. Why is it important?

* It is commanded in the Qur'an.
* It is a celebration of and thanksgiving for the Qur'an.
* It shows devotion to Allah.
* It brings Muslims closer to Allah.
* It gains forgiveness for sins.
* It fosters the brotherhood of Islam by fasting together.
* It brings awareness of what it is to be poor.

Islam uses a lunar calendar so the months move through the seasons

The **lunar calendar** causes problems for Muslims living far from the equator when Ramadan falls in summer.

Id-ul-fit'r

The ending of the fast is celebrated by the feast of Id-ul-Fit'r.

On this day, Muslims wear new clothes and go to the mosque for a special service.

After the salah, the imam gives a sermon about the benefits of Ramadan, then Muslims give their **Id zakah** to the mosque.

After this they visit each other and eat special foods and often the children are given presents. Some Muslims exchange **Id cards**.

However, Id is not a festival like Christmas and Easter. It is Ramadan that is important. Muslims must keep Ramadan, but they do not need to observe Id.

Muslims from the Indian subcontinent spell it **Eid.**

Holy days and religious taxes

Does Islam have a holy day?

Although Friday is the Muslim holy day, it is not a complete day. After midday prayers Muslims can go back to work. They need only a couple of hours off work.

Friday prayers are called **juma'h** prayers:

1 They are held at midday.
2 They must be said in the mosque.

The prayer leader (**imam**) gives a sermon (**khutbah**) that explains Islam for today.

Some mosques allow women to attend juma'h in the gallery, others encourage them to be said at home.

What is Zakah?

Zakah is a compulsory charity tax commanded in the Qur'an:

* It must be paid once a year.
* It comprises 2.5% on savings and 2.5% on income above the **nisab** (the amount needed to live on).
* Most Muslims pay the tax to the mosque to distribute.
* Special zakah should be paid on the Ids.

Zakah should be used:

* to help the poor
* to help orphans and widows
* to pay for the upkeep of mosques and Muslim schools
* to pay for Muslim missionary work.

Muslims should also pay **sadaqah** (voluntary charity) to the poor and needy.

Hajj

Hajj is the pilgrimage to **Makkah** in the month of **Dhu al'Hijja**, following the example of the Prophet's pilgrimages.

What pilgrims do	Why they do it
Circle the Ka'aba seven times	Remembering Adam, who built the Ka'aba
Run between the hills of Marwa and Sa'fa	Remembering Ismail's mother's search for water
Collect water from the Zamzam well	Remembering Ismail, who discovered the well
Confess their sins to Allah at Arafat	Sins already there will not count at the final judgement
Throw 49 stones at the pillars of stoning in Mina	Remembering how Ibrahim stoned the Devil
Sacrifice a sheep or goat and share the meat with the poor	Remembering how Ibrahim was prepared to sacrifice his son Ismail

Why is Hajj important?

* It is the Fifth Pillar.
* Muhammad went on Hajj.
* It makes Muslims realize that Islam came from Adam, and Ibrahim came before Muhammad.
* It brings Muslims close to Allah.
* It makes pilgrims aware of the power and unity of Islam.
* Other Muslims regard **Hajjis** as very holy people.
* If pilgrims die on Hajj, they go straight to heaven.

The celebration of Id-ul-Adha

At mosques all over the world there is a congregational prayer, as on Id-ul-Fit'r. Then families gather together to make their sacrifice and eat it as a celebratory meal. Instead of sharing the leftover meat with the poor, they pay the Id zakah.

Festivals and mosques

Are there other festivals?

Sunnis not affected by Wahhabism often celebrate:

* the Prophet's birthday (**mawlid**) with large street processions and stories about the life of Muhammad
* the New Year by thinking about Muhammad's emigration from Makkah and making new beginnings.

Shi'as celebrate:

* **Al'Ashura** with passion plays remembering the martyrdom of Imam Husayn
* **Ghadir al'Khum** remembering the appointment of Ali as first imam by Muhammad.

The Shi'a festivals often provoke attacks from Sunni Muslims as they condemn Sunni leadership.

What are the main features of a mosque?

* Prayer hall – mosques are often called **masjid**, which means 'place of prostration'.
* Dome – the dome is a feature of buildings in the Middle East to provide air conditioning.
* Separate prayer room for women – men and women must not pray together.
* **Minaret** – for the **muezzin** to call Muslims to prayer.
* **Mihrab** – an indicator of the direction of Makkah.
* Washrooms – for washing before salah (**wudu**).
* Carpet with lines – to pray in rows in a clean place.
* **Minbar** – a pulpit for the Friday sermon (**khutbah**).
* Shoe rack – shoes have to be removed.
* Prayer time board.
* Zakah box.
* Qur'ans on Qur'an stands.

5 Rites of passage

Rites of passage in Islam

In this chapter we shall be looking at how and why Muslims celebrate rites of passage. Muslims celebrate:

1 **Birth** – with special birth rituals and sometimes naming ceremonies; circumcision for all Muslim boys.
2 **Marriage** – with special ceremonies for the signing of the contract.
3 **Death** – with special funeral ceremonies at the mosque, and special ceremonies at the burial.

Important events in life are important also for Islam

....

What happens when a child is born?

1 As soon as a baby is born:
   a The call to prayer is recited in its right ear.
   b The call to begin to pray is recited in its left ear.

This ensures that the baby knows Allah's name and the need for prayer.

2 A week or so later there is a naming ceremony (**aqiqa**) when:
   a In some communities the child's hair is shaved and money equivalent to the weight of the hair in gold is given to the poor.
   b In others a sheep or goat is sacrificed, and the meat shared with the poor in a special meal.

3 Muslim boys are circumcised because the prophets were circumcised.

Coming of age and marriage

Are there special coming of age ceremonies?

There are no special ceremonies but boys and girls take on adult responsibilities at the onset of puberty:

* Boys and girls are no longer allowed to mix socially (except for close relatives).
* Girls must follow Islamic dress codes and wear the **hijab**.
* Boys and girls are expected to take their religious duties seriously.
* Boys are expected to attend **juma'h** prayers.
* Girls and boys are expected to pay **zakah** (or at least to work out why they do not need to pay it).

52

Why marriage?

Muslims believe that sex outside marriage is wrong because:

* Sex before marriage is forbidden by the Qur'an.
* The Shari'ah says that sex should take place only within marriage.
* Islam teaches that sex is for the procreation of children who should be raised in a family in which the mother and father are married.

Islam teaches that marriage was created by Allah so that a couple can:

* share love and companionship
* have the gift of children
* bring up a Muslim family
* follow the example of the Prophet Muhammad.

Marriage and divorce

Marriage

Muslim marriages do not have to be arranged.

Admittedly, restrictions on members of the opposite sex socializing make finding partners difficult, but Internet Muslim marriage sites have made it possible.

A Muslim wedding must involve the couple declaring, in front of witnesses, that they are marrying freely. They then sign the marriage contract, which specifies the **mahr** to be kept in trust for the bride by the groom.

Mahr: a sum of money to be paid to the bride by the groom if the marriage fails – dowries are not allowed.

There may be readings from the Qur'an and a short talk by the imam on the nature of marriage. Some weddings also include an exchange of vows.

Why divorce?

Most Muslims believe that divorce should be allowed because:

* The Qur'an permits divorce.
* The Qur'an sets out terms for custody of children and care of divorced wives.
* The Shari'ah permits divorce.
* Islam has many laws about how divorce and remarriage should operate.
* Marriage is a contract in Islam, and the contract states what should happen if the couple divorce, so divorce must be allowed.
* The Prophet Muhammad was divorced, and he is the example for Muslims.

Muslims should marry to follow Muhammad's example

Divorce and death

Why not divorce?

Some Muslims would not divorce because:

* Muhammad is reported to have said that divorce is the most hated of lawful things.
* Most marriages are arranged by families, so there is family pressure against divorce.
* Many Muslims believe that they will be sent to hell if they harm their children, and divorce is likely to harm the children.
* The Qur'an teaches that families should try to rescue the marriage before they divorce.

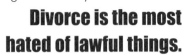

Divorce is the most hated of lawful things.

Hadith attributed to Muhammad

Death rituals

1 Before death

If it is known that someone is dying:

* Relatives and friends should be with the dying.
* The **Shahadah** should be said to them.
* Special Qur'anic verses (which Muhammad recommended as giving grace to the dying) should be said.

2 Immediately after death

* There should be no loud crying because Muhammad said that this helps the Devil to enter the house.
* The body should be prepared for burial by close relatives of the same sex. The contents of the stomach should be squeezed out and the body wrapped in white cloth leaving the face uncovered.
* Postmortems should be avoided, so that the whole body is ready for resurrection on the Last Day.

Funerals and remembering the dead

Funerals

The funeral (**janazah** prayers) should be held as soon as possible, preferably within 24 or 48 hours of the death.

The funeral should be held in the mosque:

* The prayer leader stands in front of the body facing the **qibla** and gives a short talk about the deceased.
* **Salah** is made with everyone standing in rows – but there is no prostration.

The funeral should be followed by burial in a cemetery (cremation is not allowed):

* The coffin must be buried facing Makkah.
* Prayers are said as the coffin is lowered into the grave.
* The headstone should be very simple as all Muslims are equal.

Traditionally only men attend as tears are not allowed.

Remembering the dead

On the third day after the death, family and friends meet in the house of the deceased to read from the Qur'an and say special prayers for the deceased.

Then for 40 days there can be no celebrations in the immediate family (even if it is the **Ids**). On the 40th day the prayers are said again, and the mourning is over.

There are many different traditions regarding what happens to the dead person between death and the Last Day (this period is known as **barzakh**).

Some Muslims believe that the soul hovers over the grave until the **Last Day**, and they visit the grave on the Ids to celebrate with the deceased.

6 Issues of life and death

The sanctity of life

All Muslims believe that life is a gift from Allah and therefore sacred.

This causes problems when they have to deal with such life and death issues as abortion, contraception, fertility treatments and euthanasia.

Muslims have different views on these issues depending on which Law School they follow, whether they are traditionalists or modernizers and whether they are members of a group such as the Wahhabis.

The sanctity of life means that Muslims must respect life

This chapter looks at the problems caused for Muslims by:

* the legality of abortion in many countries
* the legality of artificial methods of contraception
* the legalization of fertility treatments such as **in vitro fertilization (IVF)** and egg and sperm donation
* laws treating **euthanasia** as murder, except for withdrawing artificial feeding or treatment.

> **Kill not your children on a plea of want. We provide sustenance for you and for them; come not nigh to shameful deeds.**
>
> Qur'an 6:151

Abortion

Why are some Muslims against abortion?

Some Muslims believe that abortion should never be allowed because:

* They believe that the soul is given at the moment of conception.
* If life begins at conception, then abortion is taking life, which is murder.
* They believe that the Qur'an bans abortion.

Some Muslims believe that abortion is wrong, and should never be allowed unless the life of the mother is at risk, because:

* The death of the unborn child is a lesser evil than the death of the mother.
* The Shari'ah says that the mother's life must always take priority over that of the baby.

64

Why do some Muslims allow abortion?

Many Muslims believe that abortion must be allowed in certain circumstances (such as adverse effects on the health of mother or baby, the baby being born handicapped) because:

1 Some **hadith** say that a foetus does not become life until 120 days of pregnancy.
2 The **Shari'ah** says that the mother's life must always take priority.

They believe that, up to 120 days, if there is a risk of serious effects on the future baby and family, an abortion can be allowed.

Contraception

Are Muslims against contraception?

Some Muslims believe that contraception is against the will of Allah and should not be used at all because:

* They believe that the Qur'an's command, 'You should not kill your children for fear of want' means a ban on contraception.
* They believe that Allah created sex for having children and so contraception is against Allah's will.
* They are opposed to abortion and so would not allow any contraceptives that acted as abortifacients.
* They believe it is the duty of Muslims to have large families.

If Allah wishes to create a child, you cannot prevent it.
Hadith attributed to Muhammad

66

When might contraception be permitted?

Some Muslims believe that it is permitted for Muslims to use contraception to limit family size and protect the mother's health because:

* There are several hadith that record that the Prophet permitted the use of **coitus interruptus** as a means of contraception.
* The Qur'an says that Allah does not place extra burdens on his followers, and contraception stops extra burdens.
* If pregnancy risks a mother's health, contraception must be allowed because Islam puts the mother's life first.
* Muslim lawyers agree that contraception is different from abortion and so should be permitted.

Fertility treatments

Islam does not have problems with infertility treatments as long as they respect marriage, do not threaten life and respect a child's right to know its parents.

Muslims' attitudes depend on the exact nature of the treatment.

Treatment	Muslim attitude
Fertility drugs	Acceptable to all Muslims as they do not threaten life
In vitro fertilization (IVF)	Accepted by most Muslims as the egg and sperm are from husband and wife Banned by those Muslims who ban abortion as the process involves destruction of embryos
Artificial insemination by husband	Accepted by most Muslims for the same reasons as IVF Banned by those who ban IVF
Artificial insemination by donor	Banned by Muslims because it denies a child's right to know its parents and is regarded as a form of adultery

Treatment	Muslim attitude
Egg donation – an unknown woman's egg and the husband's sperm **Embryo donation** – both sperm and egg are from unknown donors **Surrogacy** – either the egg and sperm of husband and wife, or the egg or sperm of husband or wife and an unknown donor, are fertilized by IVF and brought to birth in another woman's womb	All of these are banned by Muslims as they deny a child's right to know its parents and are regarded as a form of adultery

Adoption is not an option for Muslims

Euthanasia

All Muslims are against euthanasia, but there are two slightly different attitudes:

1 Most are against all forms of euthanasia because:
   a The Qur'an bans suicide and so assisted suicide is wrong.
   b Most Muslims believe that voluntary euthanasia is just the same as assisted suicide.
   c Euthanasia is making yourself equal with Allah, which could be the greatest sin of **shirk** (associating other things with Allah).
   d Euthanasia is the same as committing murder, which is banned by the Qur'an.
   e Muslims believe that life is a test from Allah, and so if people use euthanasia, they are cheating in the test by trying to speed it up.

70

2 Some agree that euthanasia is wrong, but think that switching off life support machines is not because:
   a Some Muslim lawyers have agreed to life support machines being switched off when there are no signs of life.
   b If someone is brain dead, Allah has already taken his or her life.

They also think that people have a right to refuse excessive treatments and that, for example, a doctor not using resuscitation methods on a terminally ill patient having a heart attack would not be performing euthanasia.

Nor can a soul die except by God's leave.

Qur'an 3:145

7 Equality and rights

Gender, ethnicity and human rights

Gender issues

Traditionalists and fundamentalists do not:

* give women equal rights
* give homosexuals equal rights.

Modernizers:

* give women equal rights
* some give homosexuals equal rights.

Ethnicity

* All Muslims oppose racism.
* All Muslims support antidiscrimination laws.

Muslims differ on gender and human rights issues, but not on ethnicity

Human rights

* The human right to freedom of religion causes problems for many Muslims.
* Rights for homosexuals and women cause problems for some Muslims.

In the following chapter, we will study these issues in more detail, focusing on:

* the role of women
* homosexuality
* racial harmony
* human rights.

The role of women

What do traditional Muslims think about the role of women?

Traditional Muslims believe that men and women should have different rights in life and religion. They believe that women should perform their religious duties (except **Hajj**) in the home and men should worship Allah in the mosque.

They believe this because:

* The Qur'an teaches that men should support women because Allah has given men stronger physiques.
* The Qur'an teaches that women have been created to bear children and men to provide for them.
* The Qur'an teaches that men need more money than women to be the family providers.
* It is traditional for only men to attend the mosque and to be **imams**.

What do modernizers and fundamentalists think about the role of women?

Most believe that men and women should have completely equal rights in religion and education and a few would accept female religious leaders. However, they expect women to put their family duties before their career.

They believe this because:

* Allah created men and women differently, so women bear, and so should look after, the children.
* The Qur'an teaches that men and women are equal in religion and education.
* There is evidence that Muhammad encouraged both men and women to worship in the mosque.
* There were female religious leaders during the early stages of Islam.
* They have been affected by the rise of women's rights in the West.

Homosexuality

What do most Muslims think about homosexuality?

Most Muslims believe that homosexuality is wrong because:

* Homosexuality is condemned by the Qur'an, and the Qur'an is the final word of God.
* The Prophet Muhammad condemned homosexuality in several **hadith**.
* God says in the Qur'an that marriage between a man and a woman is the only lawful form of sex.
* Islam teaches that any sexual activity should have the possibility of creating children.
* All Muslims should try to have a family, but homosexuals cannot.

Many Muslims believe that it is impossible to be both Muslim and homosexual and so have declared that there are no homosexuals in Islam.

Why do some Muslims accept homosexuality?

Some Muslims believe that homosexuality is acceptable because:

* They believe that Islam is a religion of tolerance, not hate.
* They believe that Allah created and loves all people, whatever their sexual orientation.
* They believe that scientific evidence about homosexuality means that Allah must have made some people homosexual.

Some very liberal Muslims welcome civil partnerships because:

* They believe that homosexual Muslim couples should have lifelong faithful relationships just like heterosexual Muslims.

If two men among you are guilty of lewdness, punish them both.

Qur'an 4:16

Racial harmony

Why do Muslims try to promote racial harmony?

There are many reasons why Muslims should try to promote racial harmony:

* The Qur'an teaches that Allah created the whole of humanity from one pair of humans, therefore all races are related and none can be regarded as superior.
* In his final sermon, Muhammad said that every Muslim is a brother to every other Muslim.
* Muslims should follow the example of Muhammad, who promoted racial harmony.
* Islam itself has members in most ethnic groups and most countries around the world.
* Islam teaches that all Muslims form one brotherhood, the **Ummah**.

All Muslims are one family regardless of race

How do Muslims promote racial harmony?

1 Muslim national groups work with official bodies to help implement the **Race Relations Act**.

2 Muslim national groups help to ensure that the **Racial and Religious Hatred Act** does not impinge on freedom of religious expression.

3 Muslim national groups work with the **Equality and Human Rights Commission** to promote equality and human rights for all.

4 Local Muslim groups go into schools, churches, etc. to help understanding, join in police and council multiracial initiatives, and educate Muslims in their area on the needs for racial harmony and community cohesion.

5 Muslim leaders are working to recruit imams from native-born Muslims to make it easier for mosques to integrate with the local community.

Human rights

Why are human rights important for Muslims?

Freedom of thought, conscience and religion, expression, and assembly and association are essential. Muslims must have the right to:

* believe in Islam
* share their beliefs with others
* meet for worship
* have **halal** slaughtering facilities.

The right to life is a basic Muslim belief, because of their belief that life is holy and belongs to Allah.

It is also an essential human right for religious people not to be disadvantaged compared with others.

Why do human rights cause problems for Muslims?

1 Many Muslims believe that homosexuals should not have the right to form civil partnerships because homosexuality is against the will of Allah.

2 Many do not think that people should have the right to marry a person from a different faith, believing that Muslims should marry only Muslims so that the children are brought up as Muslims.

3 Most do not think that homosexuals should have the right to raise a family, believing that Muslims should be brought up by a mother and a father.

4 Islam says that Muslims should not be allowed to give up their faith. **Apostasy** is punishable by death in the Qur'an, clearly denying the right to freedom of religion.

8 Creation and the environment

Issues of creation and the environment

In this chapter we will study the relationship between Muslims and modern science:

1 How can the scientific view of creation fit with the traditional Muslim view?
2 If science can explain everything, what happens to the role of Allah?
3 Should science be allowed to alter the genetic make-up of organisms?
4 What should be the relationship of Muslims to the environment?

Science is a major area of disagreement for Muslims

Much of modern science comes from the work of Muslim scientists in the early Middle Ages who discovered and developed, for example:

* the number system
* algebra and trigonometry
* the basics of chemistry
* the diagnostic method in medicine
* the connection between dirt and disease.

Then, in the sixteenth century Muslim leaders began to criticize science, with the result that today some Muslims think that science:

* is evil and corrupts Muslims
* can be used, but absolute truth comes from Islam.

But some Muslims think that science is a way to Allah.

Islam and creation

The traditional view

Traditional Muslims believe that Allah created the earth, the heavens and life itself in six days.

> **Your Guardian-Lord is Allah, who created the heavens and the earth in six days.**
>
> Surah 7:54

The Qur'an states that Allah:

* created the sun, moon, stars and planets
* separated night from day
* created birds, fish and animals
* created Adam as the first human being and the **khalifah** of the earth.

Clearly this contradicts modern science, but Muslims who believe in the traditional view tend to ignore the scientific view.

The modernizer view

Modernizers and fundamentalists believe that the **Big Bang** and evolution were the way Allah used to create humans because:

* The Big Bang had to happen at exactly the right time.
* The way stars are formed implies a creator organizing things.
* The way that life began on earth could not have happened by chance.
* The nature of matter and the laws of science mean that, at the moment of the Big Bang, humans were bound to appear.

Islam and the environment

What Muslims believe about looking after Allah's creation

Islam teaches that:

* Allah created Adam as his **khalifah** (someone who looks after things).
* All Muslims are also Allah's khalifahs, who have to keep the balance of creation and look after the earth for Allah in the way set out in the Qur'an and the Shari'ah.
* Everyone will be judged by Allah on the way they have looked after the earth and the life on earth.
* This life is a test from Allah, a main part of which is looking after the environment in the way of Islam.
* Those who pass the test will go to paradise.
* Those who fail the test will be punished.

The earth is precious because Allah created it

90

How do these beliefs affect Muslim attitudes to environmental issues?

Belief	Effect
Allah's khalifah	Try to reduce pollution and preserve resources
The Shari'ah says that Muslims should treat animals and land kindly	Work for animal rights, make less use of fertilizers and pesticides, etc.
The Shari'ah says that Muslims should leave the earth better than found	Recycle as much as possible, use renewable resources and reduce dependence on finite resources
The Shari'ah says that Muslims should share resources fairly	Share in and support the work of groups trying to share the earth's resources more fairly and improve the standard of living in less economically developed countries without causing pollution
Stewardship is the basis of judgement	Live as good stewards, remembering that the final judgement will be on their carbon footprint

Muslims and the environment

Environmental problems

The issue of stewardship has become more urgent for Muslims because of:

1 **Climate change**
   a A major problem that could mean that some towns and cities near the sea will disappear under water.
   b Most scientists think that this change is caused by people putting too much carbon into the atmosphere.

2 **Resources**
   a A problem because non-renewable resources such as oil, natural gas and metals will disappear.
   b If not tackled, this will lead to major problems in our lifestyles.

3 **Pollution**
   a High-level carbon emissions cause climate change and acid rain.
   b Human waste (refuse and sewage) and radioactive waste from nuclear power plants can cause major health problems.

How Muslims are trying to deal with these problems

1 Groups such as **Muslim Aid** and **Islamic Relief**:
   a campaign to make governments take action on the environment
   b encourage native farmers to develop environmentally friendly alternative farming methods.

2 Groups such as the **Islamic Foundation for Ecology and Environmental Sciences**:
   a help mosques and Islamic centres to become more eco-friendly
   b give Muslims eco-friendly advice.

3 Groups such as **Green Prophet** publicize and develop for Muslim countries:
   a clean technology start-ups and investments
   b green design
   c sustainable architecture
   d energy news.

Genetic engineering

Why do many Muslims reject genetic engineering?

Most genetic research has been based on:

* allowing cells that transmit information from one generation to the next to be changed
* techniques to remove defective genes from embryos
* cloning processes to grow healthy cells to replace the diseased ones
* creating **cybrids** (human–animal embryos).

Clearly this is creating life that some Muslims oppose because they believe that:

* Only Allah should create the genetic make-up of people.
* Creating life is trying to be Allah, which is the greatest sin for Muslims.
* The processes involve killing an embryo, which is murdering human life.
* Several genetic research methods are banned by the Shari'ah.

Why do some Muslims accept genetic engineering?

Some Muslims support genetic engineering because they believe that:

* Allah created human minds to discover more about his creation.
* Genetic engineering offers the prospect of cures for currently incurable diseases.
* Muslims should do all they can to cure disease.
* Finding genetic cures is no different from finding drug cures.
* There is a difference between creating cells and creating people.
* Cloning using animal eggs, as in **cybrids**, does not involve any loss of human life.

9 Practising Islam in a non-Muslim society

Challenges for Muslims

As Islam is a religion in which civil and religious law should be the same, Muslims living in a non-Muslim society often feel that they face problems with:

* dress and food laws
* avoiding alcohol and gambling
* avoiding paying or receiving interest
* work and education.

Many Muslims feel that it is a problem when Shari'ah is not the law of the land

In this chapter we will study the problems that can face Muslims in a non-Muslim society.

Are problems caused by dress laws?

The basic principle lying behind the dress laws of Islam is that clothing should not permit any sexual attraction outside the home:

* Women should cover their whole body from neck to ankles and head and hair when outside the home.
* Men should be covered from knee to waist and not wear silk or gold.
* Neither should wear clothes normally worn by the opposite sex.
* Muslims must never appear naked before anyone else except for medical purposes.

These rules only cause problems for Muslims who interpret them as meaning that they should wear Asian/Arab/African cultural dress or who attend schools that insist on communal showers.

Food and drink

Does food cause problems?

Muslims have very strict regulations about what they can and cannot eat. Muslims are not allowed to eat:

* meat that is not **halal** (from an animal slaughtered by having its throat slit and the blood drained from it)
* any form of pork
* any animals that live on dead meat, e.g. crows, hyenas, shellfish.

The easy way to avoid any problems in this area is for Muslims to become vegetarian, but, if living in a Jewish area, they can eat **kosher**.

What about Islam and alcohol?

O ye who believe! Intoxicants and gambling ... are an abomination of Satan's handiwork; eschew such abominations.

Qur'an 5:93-4

Muslims are not allowed to drink alcohol or have anything to do with its manufacture or sale because it is banned by the Qur'an and **hadith**.

However, Muslims are allowed to take medicines, prescribed by a doctor, that contain alcohol or other drugs.

Some Muslims find this a problem in Western society because drinking alcohol is so much a part of the social norm, and not drinking cuts them out of some activities.

Some find it a problem in avoiding selling alcohol when running a small shop.

Interest and the use of money

Why does charging interest cause problems?

The Qur'an bans Muslims from being involved in **riba** – the lending of money at interest. It states that those who lend or borrow at interest will go to hell.

Muslims believe that riba is wrong because interest takes money from the poor and gives it to the rich, whereas Islam should take money from the rich and give it to the poor.

This causes problems for Muslims living in non-Muslim societies because they cannot:

* have mortgages
* buy things on hire purchase
* use credit cards
* have savings accounts in banks or building societies
* have interest-paying current accounts
* take out loans.

102

Good Muslims should not use capitalist banks

How do Muslims deal with the problem of interest?

Problem	Solution
Current accounts and savings accounts	Only use Muslim banks, which give a share of profits rather than charging or giving interest Use Western banks that have special Muslim facilities approved by the **ulama**
Mortgages	Form savings groups so that houses can be bought one at a time without involving anyone in mortgages
Loans and hire purchase	Save for things so that cash can be paid
Credit cards	Use debit cards, which are accepted in just as many places but do not charge interest

Some Muslims solve the problem by using non-interest-bearing current accounts, but use mortgages and credit cards because they think that paying interest is not as bad as receiving it.

Education and work

What problems does education cause?

In all Western societies, children have to be educated until at least aged 16. This usually takes place in state schools, and Muslim parents worry about:

* mixed-sex classes after the age of puberty
* science being taught as more important than religion
* Islam not being taught
* Christianity being taught
* making friends with non-Muslims
* children wanting to marry a non-Muslim.

Their concern is that education will Westernize children and encourage them to turn their backs on Islam.

What problems does work cause?

Finding suitable work in a non-Muslim society can be difficult because Muslims should not work in jobs that are un-Islamic, e.g. any jobs having connections with alcohol, gambling or sex.

Employers may:

* find it difficult to make provision for prayer times, especially as they vary throughout the year with sunrise and sunset
* not be able to give time off for Friday prayers, which all Muslims should attend
* not be sympathetic to the problems of fasting in Ramadan, especially not drinking when Ramadan falls in the summer
* not be prepared to give time off for the **Id celebrations**.

Muslim responses

How do Muslims deal with the problems of education and work?

Problem	Solution
Mixed-sex classes	Choose single-sex school or negotiate school uniform
Islam not being taught	Have classes at the mosque
Children making friends with non-Muslims	Have social activities at the mosque
Children wanting to marry a non-Muslim	Bring them up assuming that they will marry a Muslim
Working in jobs that are un-Islamic	Set up own business
No provision for prayer times	Make sure own business is flexible, e.g. taxi, market stall *Or* combine prayer times
No time off for Friday prayers, no support with fasting in Ramadan	Flexible own business
No time off for the Id celebrations	Flexible own business

What about gambling?

Gambling is prohibited by the Qur'an, and so Muslims should not bet. This includes:

* any betting on horses, football, etc.
* buying lottery tickets
* buying raffle tickets
* premium bonds
* making money by buying and selling shares rather than investing in companies.

There is debate in Islam as to whether all games of chance are forbidden (e.g. card games, Monopoly, etc., which do not involve gambling) because the Qur'an says that Muslims should not be involved in things that depend on luck.

10 War, punishment and living in a multifaith society

Muslim attitudes

War

* Most believe that they can fight just wars.
* Some are **pacifists** and will not fight.

Punishment

* Some agree with the **hadd** punishments of Islam.
* Others think that punishment should be **reformative**.

Other religions

* Some believe that only Islam has the truth.
* Others believe that other religions have some truth.

Muslims are divided on all these issues

What do Muslims mean by a just war?

Most Muslims agree that a war is just if:

* The cause is just (for example, it is fought in self-defence).
* It is fought under the authority of the UN.
* It is fought because Islam is being attacked.
* It is fought to bring back peace.
* It is a last resort – all other ways of ending the conflict have failed.
* There is a reasonable chance of success.
* The methods used avoid killing civilians.
* The methods used are proportional to the cause.

In this chapter we will study Muslim attitudes to war and punishment, and issues raised by multifaith societies.

It would not be just to destroy a country with nuclear weapons because it had invaded a small island.

Fighting in wars

Why do most Muslims believe they can fight in just wars?

Peace is the ideal for Muslims, as one of the meanings of Islam is peace. However, most Muslims believe that they should fight in just wars because:

* The Qur'an says that Muslims must fight if they are attacked.
* Muhammad fought in wars.
* There are many **hadith** from Muhammad saying that Muslims should fight in just wars.
* The Qur'an says that Muslims dying in a just war will go straight to heaven.

112

Why do some Muslims refuse to fight in wars?

Some Muslims feel that no modern war can be just because:

* There is no longer a Muslim empire, so no one has the authority to declare a war to be just.
* The methods of modern warfare are bound to affect innocent civilians, and so they cannot be just.
* The existence of weapons of mass destruction means that the methods can never be proportionate.

They also believe that:

* The evidence of history is that fighting wars does not bring lasting peace.
* Lasting peace can come only when people refuse to fight in wars.

They also look to a **hadith** of Muhammad when he said:

'War is a deception.'

Punishment

What do Muslims think about punishment?

Muslim attitudes to punishment are based on deterrence, retribution and reform. The Qur'an sets out certain punishments known as the **hadd punishments**:

* Thieves should have a hand amputated.
* Those committing adultery or drinking alcohol should be whipped.
* Homosexuals should be stoned.

The threat of this is believed to deter people from crime, and the punishment will reform, for example, thieves because they will always be aware of what has happened to them and will not want to risk it happening again.

It is also possible in Islam for a criminal to pay compensation to the victim, or the victim's family, for certain crimes. This is done as a form of **retribution**.

Why do Muslims disagree about the hadd punishments?

Why some agree	Why some disagree
The Qur'an sets down lashes or amputation for certain crimes	If a wrong verdict is given, judges cannot put a hand back on
Whipping and amputation allow the offender to remain in society with their families where they are less likely to reoffend	Countries that do not use the hadd punishments have a lower crime rate, showing that they do not deter
The idea of deterrence requires very severe punishment to work	The hadd punishments deny some human rights
The strict punishments are given only as a last resort	Amputation makes it difficult for criminals to start a new life

Seeking converts

What do Muslims think about converting other religions?

Some Muslims feel that it is their duty to convert the world to Islam, because only by being Muslim can people enjoy this life and the next.

> ## Again and again will those who disbelieve wish that they had bowed in Islam.
>
> Qur'an 15.2

These Muslims have missionary groups that are actively trying to convert Western countries to Islam, for example:

* The Islamic Propagation Centre distributes Qur'ans and pamphlets.
* The True Religion is a website about converts to Islam.

Muslims believe that Islam is the only true religion

What do other Muslims believe?

Some other Muslims believe that they should simply work at being a good Muslim and let other people get on with their own religion.

They have groups such as the British Muslim Forum working with other religions to try to discover what is the same in their religions (e.g. Judaism, Islam and Christianity believe in the prophets Abraham and Moses), and, from this, work out ways of living together without trying to convert each other.

Some **imams** and mosques are working with the Inter Faith Network for the UK to promote good relations between people of different faiths in this country.

Muslim groups such as **Da'watul Islam UK/Eire** bring together the different religious groups in an area to promote community cohesion between them.

What do Muslims think about other religions?

What do most Muslims believe?

Most Muslims believe that, although other religions have a right to exist, they are wrong and will not go to heaven. They believe that Muslims have a duty to convert other religions to Islam so that everyone goes to heaven.

They believe this because the Qur'an teaches that:

* Muhammad was given Allah's final and perfect revelation.
* Only Muslims will go to heaven.
* Muslims should try to convert all non-Muslims to Islam.

What do some other Muslims believe?

Some other Muslims believe that, although Islam is the only religion that has the full truth, Judaism and Christianity may lead people to God:

* The Qur'an says that no one should be forced into believing or following a religion.
* The Qur'an gives special mention to Jews and Christians.
* Islam teaches that Allah has sent many messengers whose message has been distorted.

A few Muslims believe that there is truth in all religions, and each religion is just a different path to the same god because:

* The Qur'an teaches that Allah is all-merciful.
* Many Sufi Muslim leaders have said that Allah can be found in different ways.